POMPEII
and
HERCULANEUM

The art and life of
POMPEII
and
HERCULANEUM

By Michael Grant

Newsweek Books, New York

This painting of a *Young Woman with Stylus and Writing Tablet* found in Pompeii is a superb example of Roman portraiture, dating from ca. 50 A.D. (Naples National Museum).

Editorial Director: Henry A. La Farge
Editorial Associate: Gemma Verchi

Published by
NEWSWEEK, INC.
& ARNOLDO MONDADORI EDITORE

ISBN, 0–88225–269–0
Library of Congress Card No. 78–65505
©1979–Arnoldo Mondadori Editore–CEAM–Milan
All rights reserved. Printed and bound in Italy
by Arnoldo Mondadori, Verona

Frontispiece
A Small Temple with people making offerings at an altar, mural painting in the Fourth Style, from Pompeii. (Naples, National Museum).

INTRODUCTION

by Michael Grant

In the eighteenth century, when Pompeii and Herculaneum were being rediscovered, it was declared that "the grand object of all travel is to see the shores of the Mediterranean." The sage, Dr. Samuel Johnson, who made this assertion, was accustomed to making pontifical statements, and some have thought that here he was going rather too far. Yet, despite pollution, despite politics, many stretches of these shorelands still retain an unequaled beauty. And perhaps the most beautiful region of all (and the most fertile as well) is Campania is southwestern Italy. The coastline of this land, which begins some ninety miles southeast of Rome, includes the incomparable Bay of Naples. Above the bay rises Mount Vesuvius, which is more formidable than its height of under 4,200 feet suggests. West of Vesuvius is Naples itself, while the remains of Herculaneum stand to the southwest of the mountain, and Pompeii to its southeast. Naples was already a great town in ancient times—but Pompeii and Herculaneum were relatively small, numbering some 25,000 and 5,000 inhabitants respectively.

Naples was founded by the Greeks (ca. 650 B.C.), who called it Neapolis, the New City; they colonized this entire coastal area, and settled at both Pompeii and Herculaneum, or had trading posts there. Subsequently these two smaller towns (though never Naples itself), fell under the temporary influence of one or more of the powerful Etruscan city-states which lay northwest of the still relatively minor power of Rome. In the fifth century B.C., the dominant role in the area fell to the Samnites, tough Italian hillsmen who came from fortified strongpoints in the center of the peninsula. But Rome, now rising rapidly, defeated the Samnites, and annexed Campania—which became their first window upon the Mediterranean. In this process, they took over Pompeii and Herculaneum (310-302 B.C.), though as was their wise practice, these towns were no doubt left to govern themselves. Nevertheless, in 91 B.C., both Pompeii and Herculaneum joined a violent Italian rebellion against Roman domination. But they were apparently reduced by the Roman general Sulla, who, when he later became dictator, made Pompeii a "colony," injecting a draft of Roman settlers but leaving the place's autonomy intact under a new system of government.

After that, Pompeii enjoyed another century and a half of peaceful existence and prosperous growth. A harbor town alongside the small river Sarnus (Sarno), serving a rich inland zone, it was also a small but bustling center of wine and oil production (although Pompeian wine was said to give one a hangover); its local industries included wool and woolen goods, and it exported a famous fish-sauce (see note at end), fruit, volcanic stone (tufa) and millstones.

For a long time Vesuvius had remained quiet. Indeed, it had never erupted since the beginning of recorded history, though Strabo, a Greek geographer at the turn of our era, rightly deduced from its appearance that the crater had once been volcanic. A warning was given (though not heeded) in the reign of Nero, during the month of February A.D. 62, when a severe earthquake badly damaged the towns around the mountain, Pompeii worse than any of them. The damage was so severe that, when the fatal eruption took place seventeen years later, only a very few of the town's public and private buildings had by then been fully restored.

The eruption took place in A.D. 79—soon after the accession of the emperor Titus—so that we are now celebrating its nineteen hundredth anniversary. August 24, A.D. 79, dawned clear and hot. There had been earth tremors for several days, and springs had dried up, but probably no one was particularly worried. Then came the sudden, appalling explosion. We can tell more or less what took place from analyses of the deposits which buried the whole region, and from a famous account by Pliny the younger, the literary nephew of the famous encyclopaedist and historian of the same name. The latter personage, the elder Pliny, happened at the time to be the commander of the Roman fleet at Misenum (Miseno), nineteen miles away at the northwestern end of the Bay of Naples. His nephew was with him, and in later years wrote his eyewitness recollections of the eruption in two letters to the historian Tacitus. A vast dark cloud had appeared across the bay, and had blotted out the sun. "Its general appearance can best be expressed as being like an [umbrella] pine rather than any other tree, for it rose to a great height on a sort of trunk and then split off into branches, I imagine because it was thrust upwards by the first blast and then left unsupported as the pressure subsided, or else it was borne down by its own weight so that it spread out and gradually dispersed. Sometimes it looked white, sometimes blotched and dirty, according to the amount of soil and ashes it carried with it."

The elder Pliny, receiving a desperate message from a woman friend along the coast, ordered the warships out (his nephew is careful to point out that it was not for her sake alone), and made for a point near Herculaneum, west of the volcano. But bad conditions and falls of debris made it impossible for him to land, and he sailed on instead to Stabiae (Castellamare di Stabia, south of Vesuvius), where he spent the night at a friend's villa near the sea. On the following morning, however, Pliny, who was a fat man, was overcome by fumes on the beach, and fell down and died. It was not until two days of pitch darkness, only broken terrifyingly by lightning and the flames of electric storms, that his body could be recovered.

By that time, Pompeii had long since been obliterated. Indeed, since the eruption started in the late morning of the 24th, more than a man's height of ash must already have fallen over the city by what y would ordinarily have been sunset on the same day. The surface of solid basalt, which had plugged the cone of the volcano since before the beginning of history, was suddenly shattered by an overwhelming build-up of heat and pressure from far beneath the earth. A vast mass of lava and boulders leapt thousands of feet into the air, and crashed down like a rain of bombs, followed by an impenetrable cloud of incandescent pumice—white, grey and greyish in color—which covered the ground of Pompeii up to a height of six or eight feet. Then, in the night that followed, the sides of the old volcanic cone collapsed inward, causing a fresh series of explosive shocks which convulsed the whole region with violent earthquakes. A torrent of steam, ash, cinders and dust rose precipitously into the sky and hurtled downward again in a thick, seething mass, which blanketed the ground with an additional seven feet of deposit. It was not until late in the day of the 26th that a dim light finally reappeared to reveal a scene of unprecedented desolation.

A different fate had befallen Herculaneum, which had been overwhelmed not by pumice and ashes but by a torrid, treacly sea of mud. At least, however, the slow approach of this wave had enabled most of the population to get away in time. At Pompeii, many more people were taken by surprise, and the number of fatalities amounted to at least two thousand. The first victims were struck down by lava, rocks and falling masonry, and then many more were suffocated by ash, and, above all, asphyxiated by the sulphurous fumes and lethal chloride-impregnated gases

View of Pompeii from the Tower of Mercury. The street in the center is Mercury Street, leading from the Tower to the Forum. The paved streets, with their sidewalks, evoke the animated traffic, flourishing trade and efficient organization of city life.

that the belching crater emitted. Innumerable dramatic signs of these tragic casualties were still to be seen when the excavators came upon the site. A room in a house, where a group had taken refuge, was found closed with an iron shutter: the remains of twelve people were discovered inside. On the threshold of another house, its mistress and three of her maids lay dead, her jewelry and money scattered around. In one building, the top story crumbled and fell in ruins, killing seven children inside. The priests of the shrine of the Egyptian goddess Isis set out to seek safety, carrying with them the treasures of the temple. But one by one, at different points, they collapsed, scattering their valuables around them; the last of them to remain alive and on their feet took refuge inside a house, where one of them broke through two walls with an axe, but to no avail because he and his companions all perished.

The survival of small material objects was extraordinary and uncanny. Eggs and fish were still to be seen where there had not been time to eat them. At an eating-house, eighty-one loaves remained, carbonized, in the oven, where they had been placed only a few seconds before the building was overwhelmed. At another inn, gladiators did not have time to finish their drinks and left their trumpets behind as they fled. In their own barracks, sixty gladiators succumbed, including several in chains, as well as a richly jeweled woman who was paying one of the inmates a visit. Not many beasts of burden lost their lives in the city, because escapers had mobilized the rest to take them away. But dead dogs have been found, and one of them offers a horrible testimony, because it gnawed the adjoining dead body of its master before it, too succumbed. Outside the walls the casualties continued. In one of the extensive cemeteries in the city outskirts, thirty-four men, women and children hid themselves away in a tomb, taking with them large food supplies including a goat, but there, goat and all, they met their deaths. Efforts to get away by sea proved equally unsuccessful since, even when people managed to struggle through to the coast, scorching waves and wind made embarkation impossible.

In the very first days after the eruption, before the jumble of debris had solidified, efforts were made to salvage the valuables that lay beneath it. Parties of survivors—rescuers or robbers, or both—saved what they could, using the tallest parts of the buried buildings which still rose above the devastation, to guide them. In particular, bronze statues and marble facings in the Forum were removed. The visitors to this dreadful buried world left graffiti: one, written by a Jew or a Christian, just simply says "Sodom and Gomorrah." The emperor Titus attempted relief measures, but nothing much seems to have come of them.

During the long centuries that followed, fresh townships were gradually established near the former city of Pompeii, and the other obliterated places roundabout. But from the ancient sites there was total silence, until the eighteenth century when gradual, tentative, unsystematic discoveries began to reveal the unimaginable riches that lay far beneath the surface. The impact of these finds on the beginnings of modern Italian archaeology, on the thoughts of German writers such as Goethe, and on the interior decorators of Western Europe (where, by coincidence, artistic taste was turning toward Neo-Classicism and ready for such influences) makes a whole series of fascinating stories.

The activities of Sir William Hamilton, British envoy to the King of Naples from 1764 to 1800, are also well worth notice. Many valuable objects from Pompeii and Herculaneum found their way into his own private collection. However, he was subsequently obliged to sell a considerable number of them "because he had spent so much on Emma," his beautiful young wife, who later became the mistress of Admiral Horatio Nelson (and put on a lot of weight). Then Sir William formed a second collection, which was sunk on *H.M.S. Colossus* off the Scilly Islands in 1798. The ship has now been salvaged and the fragmentary remains of his treasures acquired in 1975 by the British Museum are now being meticulously reassembled so that they can be placed on exhibition.

A special tribute must be made to Giuseppe Fiorelli, with whose appointment to look after these sites (1860–75) systematic excavation began. It was he who first adopted the practice of restoring the old buildings in order to make them comprehensible to visitors: so that the ruined cities constitute entire museums in themselves, and museums of the most spectacular possible kind—amply justifying, it will surely be agreed, the inclusion of the present volume in the series entitled "Museums of the World." Fiorelli's desire was to preserve as many as possible of the objects that were found on the spot, instead of taking away the most

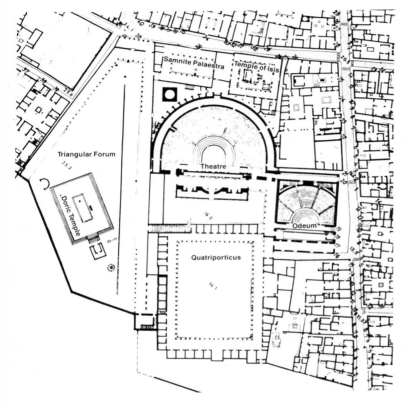

Map of the theater district

spectacular items and not caring what happened to the rest of the site (though, in today's conditions, it has proved more prudent to remove important objects to the Naples Museum). Moreover, Fiorelli invented an ingenious way of recapturing the living appearance of the people whose remains have been found at Pompeii. He noted that in many cases the ash deposit had solidified so closely around the dead bodies that, after decomposition, their forms were still exactly preserved around the empty space that had thus been created. By inserting a tube into this hollow space (after the bones had been removed), and then injecting a specially designed solution of liquid plaster, which subsequently hardened, the shape of the body was reproduced. The detailed results of this process are astonishing. Even the outlines of clothing and sandals, the traces of hair on head and face and body, are meticulously preserved; even

the facial expressions of the death agony have come down to us over 'the centuries. Only last year, the Fiorelli technique was applied once again to two new discoveries, victims of the eruption who were suffocated in an out-of-town cemetery. One of the dead was a young girl who wore silver bracelets and had taken a bronze statuette with her when she unavailingly took refuge.

This is macabre. And yet it is also touching and *enjoyable.* Its enjoyableness raises interesting problems about what sort of persons we ourselves are, and how we feel. The Japanese writer, Haruko Ichikawa, was more worried about the posthumous fate of the people who were thus so surprisingly preserved. "It would not," he said, "be very pleasant to become part of a show excavated after two thousand years." But equally relevant is the question why we ourselves find so much pleasure in the show.

However, it is a question that has to be broadened, to include the impact upon us not only of the corpses but of the entire dead city of Pompeii as it is uniquely set out for our inspection—and entertainment. "Many a calamity," said Goethe, "has happened in the world, but never one that caused so much entertainment to posterity as this one." Such "enjoyment of ruins" seemed to the novelist Henry James a heartless, perverse pleasure, and it was the *deadness* of Pompeii that struck Sir Walter Scott; as he walked around the empty streets in his old age, he muttered repeatedly "The City of the Dead! The City of the Dead!" One reason for his depression was no doubt diagnosed by his later fellow-author Malcolm Lowry, who declared that "it is as if you could hear *your own* real life plunging to its doom." Certainly, "remember that you too are mortal" is one of the messages that visitors cannot fail to carry away from the ghost site of Pompeii. But that is not all, for the real point of the site is the overpowering way in which it shows not only death, but *life and death* together, in inextricably close association. Life is in death, and death is in life; the place emits an all-pervading aura of being and not being at one and the same time.

This dualism is of course seen with the most arresting immediacy in the plaster casts of the men, women, boys and girls who were struck down and transfixed in midstride. They were ordinary human beings, people who had no doubt lived ordinary lives, but by an exceptional blow of

Map of the city of Pompeii

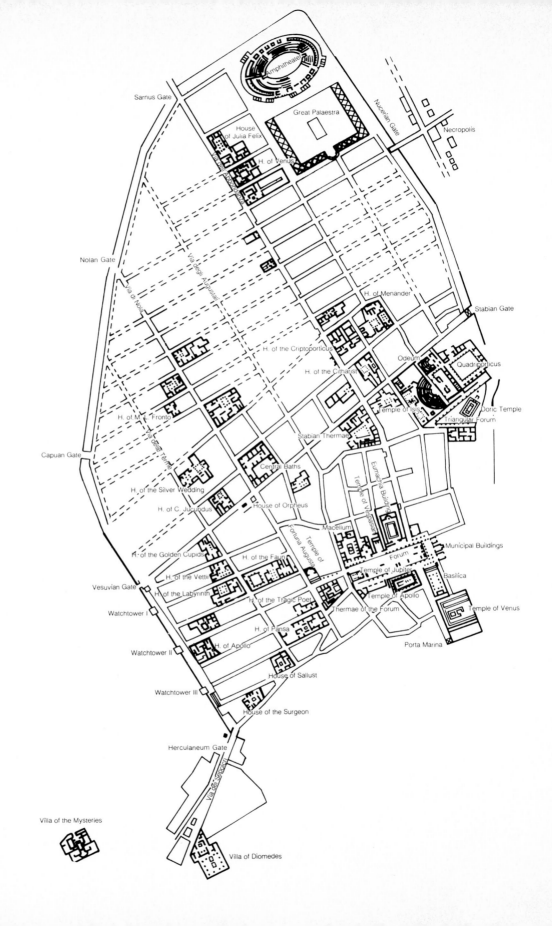

Sarnus Gate

Amphitheater

Great Palaestra

Nucerian Gate

Necropolis

House of Julia Felix

H. of Venus

Nolan Gate

Via degli Augustali

H. of Menander

Stabian Gate

Via di Nola

H. of the Criptoporticus

Odeum

Quadriporticus

H. of the Citharist

Temple of Isis

Doric Temple

H. of M. L. Fronto

Triangular Forum

Via delle Terme

Stabian Thermae

Capuan Gate

Central Baths

H. of the Silver Wedding

Eumachia Building

Temple of Vespasian

H. of C. Jucundus

House of Orpheus

Macellum

Municipal Buildings

H. of the Golden Cupids

Temple of Fortuna Augusta

Forum

H. of the Faun

Temple of Jupiter

H. of the Vettii

Basilica

Vesuvian Gate

H. of the Labyrinth

Temple of Apollo

Temple of Venus

Watchtower I

H. of the Tragic Poet

Thermae of the Forum

Watchtower II

H. of Pansa

Porta Marina

H. of Apollo

House of Sallust

Watchtower III

House of the Surgeon

Herculaneum Gate

Via dei Sepolcri

Villa of the Mysteries

Villa of Diomedes

10

fate were subjected to an extraordinary catastrophic misfortune, which has made them our companions today. It is they, the microcosms of the human condition, representatives of all humanity, who make Pompeii unique. And their uniqueness is underlined by the little piquant, everyday things in their lives which have survived alongside them: the remains of food, the schoolboy's inkpot, the dice and knuckle-bones for gambling, the lamps and bottles and jugs, the tradesman's stamp and carpenter's plane and doctor's intimate instruments, the half-finished work lying on the jeweler's bench, the garden ornaments (not to everyone's taste, but better than modern plastic gnomes), and the marble slab advising us that the freedman Januarius recommends the salt and fresh water baths of Marcus Crassus Frugi.

And then there are all those innumerable messages painted or incised on Pompeian walls. The painted inscriptions include a revealing collection of local election notices and propaganda. In contrast to Rome, where the emperor's shadow leaned more heavily, rivalry for the annually contested chief municipal offices of Pompeii remained extremely acute. At the time of the eruption, the election campaign of 79 was just heating up, and has left its mark in the pronouncements of countless canvassers. Some of these, I suspect, are really intended to work *against* the candidate they appear to favor. A certain Vatia, for example, is ostensibly supported by everyone "who is fast asleep" and "is a late drinker"—and by the pickpockets of the town. Another candidate has a rather damping testimonial: "his grandmother did a lot of hard work for him at his last election." And yet another has an indefatigable supporter in his "little girl-friend," which may not have been the best possible recommendation.

But what perhaps makes a stronger historical impact than anything else is the mass of graffiti on the walls. Unfortunately, they will offer little visual impression to the tourist, because they are just scratchy incisions, hard to see, and in any case many have now been removed to the Naples Museum, while others have just crumbled away. But first they were carefully listed, and copied; and they still have an enormous amount to yield to future research. Indeed, I doubt if there is any other single source that can tell us more about how the people of any part of the Roman Empire thought and felt.

The dark outline surrounding this *Map of Pompeii* marks the fortified wall extending more than ten thousand feet. Reconstructions and repairs were made at various times, but the original contours were never modified. In this wall perimeter are eight gates and several towers.

A huge range of human activities is represented by these graffiti—politics, literature, grass-roots religion, lavatory humor, and above all (as today) sex in alarmingly diversified abundance. Sex appears in many paintings too, notably in some of the (at least) seven brothels that this small town provided. Sex is pretty open at Pompeii, and representations of the male organ are particularly abundant. An interesting question arises. Was it like this all over the Roman empire, or was the Greek culture of this particular region especially uninhibited? Since other towns do not furnish the wealth of material evidence that we have from Pompeii, we cannot give a certain answer. But it can at least be said that Pompeii and its neighboring towns, because of their civilized backgrounds, probably present the subject with greater artistry than would have been found elsewhere.

For that is the keynote of the entire Pompeian scene, and an astringent reminder to those who believe we have improved in every way since those ancient times. That is to say, whether morals have got better or not (as is hard to tell), the general standard of aesthetic achievement in the cities of Vesuvius is a great deal higher than could be found in almost any townships of similar size in the world of today. And, by the same token, the cultural amenities Pompeii and Herculaneum offered were far more impressive than anything comparable modern towns could offer. What town of 25,000 inhabitants nowadays has two elegant stone theaters, one large and one small? And what twentieth-century town has no less than four sets of public baths—not to speak of those that still may await discovery—equipped with a wide, luxurious range of club facilities, and decorated with graceful stucco facings on their walls and vaults? Moreover, as many as ten temples have come to light at Pompeii, which must have presented a distinguished appearance when they were whole; and although their surviving remains are comparatively insubstantial, they constitute a treasure house of information about ancient religion.

As to the city's amphitheater, there is the usual contradictory judgment to offer. Like others of its kind, it served the appallingly brutal purpose of gladiatorial duels—and it is good to know that in A.D. 59, because of spectator riots, the emperor Nero closed the arena for a time. And yet, architecturally, the great external arches of this Pompeian

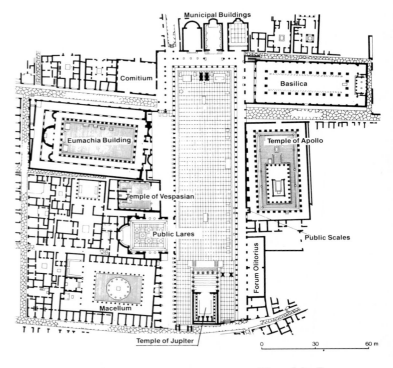

Plan of the Forum

amphitheater, and its spacious auditorium, present a fine appearance. Furthermore, it is noteworthy that here, in so small a town, we have the oldest known permanent edifice of the kind anywhere in the world dating back to 80 B.C. An impressive early date must also be attributed to Pompeii's Basilica, a term for those imposing public halls of the pagan Roman world that were the ancestors of law courts, Christian basilicas, Italian *gallerie* and stock exchanges all in one. The Basilica at Pompeii was built about 100 B.C., at a date earlier than any basilica in Rome itself that has come down to us. This is only one of innumerable ways in which Pompeii contributes vastly to our knowledge of architectural history.

The Pompeian Basilica faces the city's Forum, the type of open city square which ranks high among the great achievements of ancient Italy's architecture and town planning. Surrounded, like Greek marketplaces but more impressively, by colonnades on three sides—the fourth being reserved for the city's main temple of Jupiter—the whole composition of the Forum at Pompeii must have been delightful and stimulating: a not unworthy ancestor of the central open spaces that are the glories of later Italian cities, culminating in the Piazza San Marco at Venice. To see the Pompeii Forum empty, though, is unnatural, and to that extent today's tourists serve a purpose, because they fill the unnaturally silent vacuum. For in ancient times these *Fora,* as Lord Clark aptly puts it, were "the open squares of Latin civilization, with their resistant masonry echoing the shouts of uninhibited extroversion."

And yet it is not the public but the private buildings of Pompeii that are most informative of all about the lives of its inhabitants. One of the desirable outcomes of the most recent excavations and researches has been a much wider knowledge of the various kinds of dwellings of the under-privileged and the poor (including in the city's later years, a partitioning of the larger houses into much smaller apartments). I hope a full-scale study of this subject may before long be written, to the great advantage of our sociological knowledge of the Roman world (which has also benefited enormously from our discoveries of small shops and inns of the city, and from revelations of the remarkable social mobility the place displayed). But it is, obviously, the residences of those who were better off that have proved the more lasting; it is they that have captured the imagination of posterity. Indeed, these surviving houses of Pompeii have been described, with some justification, as the most wonderful of all the monuments that antiquity has left for our inspection anywhere in the world.

They look inward, mainly deriving their light not from external windows but from courtyards within. Any visitor on a burning Campanian summer day can admire the way in which these architects sought and realized an ideal of coolness and peace amid the hot clatterings of the outside world. The main courtyard of these houses was a rectangular "atrium" (probably borrowed from the Etruscans), usually with an opening in the middle of its roof, located above a catch basin for the collection of rain water. Around the atrium were various rooms, and behind them, if there was space enough, lay an enclosed garden court or peristyle; and the largest houses had an open garden and orchard as well.

These dwellings sometimes attained dimensions of up to 700 square yards. And yet to modern eyes some features of their design are curiously unimpressive. For example, the rooms (especially the dining rooms) are often poky and diminutive—and kitchen and toilet facilities tend to be more than sketchy. Heating (excellent in the public baths) was inadequate in private houses—for the Pompeian winter can be perishingly cold—and window panes (again in contrast to the baths) were very rare or nonexistent, so that wooden shutters had to serve instead; and the artificial lighting, by torches or tapers or tallow candles, must have been ineffectual and smelly.

On the other hand the gardens were charming; their contents have been cleverly reconstructed, again by Fiorelli's technique of pouring plaster into the vacuums left by the vanished roots. But what is most remarkable of all—and once more reminds us of the high standard of general taste—was the interior decoration of these houses. Its main principles were two: wall surfaces should be covered all over with paintings applied directly to the surfaces of the walls themselves, and floors should be similarly covered from end to end with mosaics. True, panel paintings for the walls were not unknown, and no doubt rugs were at least occasionally placed on the floors. But neither of these practices became at all common, since both seemed to ancient ideas to upset the architectural lines of the house (for the same reason, furniture was, by modern standards, sparse). So ancient Pompeii, for decade after decade, provides us with a whole succession of wall paintings and floor mosaics, and this enormously varied, chronologically recordable series is an astonishing contribution to our knowledge of the ancient world. Some of these masterpieces, not only providing copies of vanished Greek painting which are of great importance to the art historians, but also comprising works that are entirely original, are shown by reproductions in this book. The technique employed—painting on a carefully prepared surface of lime mortar topped with coats of marble dust to create a shiny, brilliant surface—was an exacting and difficult process requiring great skill.

The paintings have customarily been classified in four successive styles, though they overlap and, in the light of more recent study, the arrangement stands in need of an overhaul. But it has helped to establish the main lines of

Plaster Casts of Victims of the Eruption, who died by
suffocation. The casts were obtained by filling with liquid
plaster the hollow shapes left by the hardened lava around the
corpses. This method of reproducing the shape of bodies,
wooden objects, foodstuffs, was invented by Giuseppe Fiorelli
in 1864.

development. The earliest kind of wall painting found at Pompeii, from early in the first century B.C., is the so-called Incrustation style (from *crusta,* a slab of marble) because, like Greek work of the previous century and earlier, it simulates the color contrasts of marble, alabaster or porphyry facings used to cover walls. Then, later in the same century, came the Second, or Architectural style, in which vivid representations of buildings offer daring, three-dimensional vistas of streets, houses and colonnaded halls, apparently in imitation of stage settings for theatrical performances, and designed so as to create the illusion that the rooms are larger than they actually are. From then onward, too, paintings show charmingly skillful rural scenes and still-life representations strangely anticipating the Dutch masterpieces of a later millennium.

The Third style, which overlapped with the Second and continued until about A.D. 50, abandoned this illusionistic opening up of internal spaces, reducing the painted forms to tenuous, plant-like candelabra, vines and garlands in which the architectural character had become scarcely more than ornament against the overall ground color. The Fourth Style, which started before the Third was over and is held to have continued until the life of Pompeii came to an end, is a somewhat meaningless designation covering a considerable diversity of pictorial motifs; and by far the greater part of Pompeii's surviving paintings belong to this period. Architectural patterns—enlivened with little figures and fabulous beasts—have become even more delicately ornamental. Fashionable also were scenes in which mythological themes abound: in the best of such pictures, faces and emotions are vividly suggested by a few bold and impressionistic brushstrokes. These are sympathetic portraits of real persons— presumably the owners of the houses—which astutely catch the moods of their sitters. Romantic, idyllic pastoral countrysides are also to be found, including Egyptian river scenes and exotic menageries. The amount of skill displayed in all these different kinds of paintings varies considerably. For one thing, some house owners may not have been too particular, thinking of the pictures as symbols of social standing and financial investments rather than works of art. And, besides, artists of every quality had to be pressed into service after the earthquake of A.D. 62, which had left such a large number of houses in need of complete redecoration. All the same, the level of accomplishment displayed by many of the painters is remarkable. Their achievements remain highly distinctive; their reddish

grounds—the famous Pompeian red—stay in the mind, and so does their characteristically light and airy brushwork.

Floor mosaics, too, made up of little colored cubes of colored stone and marble arranged in beds of cement, became a typical, successful, and wonderfully durable art in Pompeii. According to the late Sir Mortimer Wheeler, it was *the* Roman art. The Greeks, in their early experiments in the medium, had envisaged these mosaic designs as alternatives to rugs in the middle of the floor spaces, or to mats beside the door. In Italy, and very notably in the Vesuvian cities, not only did this tradition continue, but another practice also arose, according to which the whole floor came to be envisaged as a single space, to be covered all over by a carpet-like mosaic of unified design. So Pompeian mosaics come in all sizes; and they include a great range of different colorful themes, manners and methods.

The most famous of the large-scale mosaics shows an elaborate scene of the Battle of Issus (333 B.C.) between Alexander the Great and the Persians, adapted from a Greek picture that is now lost. There are also innumerable other fine examples, many now in the Naples Museum along with the paintings. Among them are charming miniature mosaics, made up of particularly tiny cubes arranged in sinuously curving designs; not all of these compositions were inset in floors, some of them being mounted on marble trays. One of these miniature pieces is a strikingly effective female portrait; others show theatrical groupings. A mosaic displaying an unswept dining room floor must have served as an admonition to careless diners (as did messages painted on a dining room wall urging them to behave themselves respectably during the meal—such as are found in the House of the Moralist). Equally startling is the depiction of a fight between an octopus and a lobster, intended for the floor of a pool or a bath. Mosaics were also beginning to creep up from the floors to the walls and vaults upon which, centuries later, they were to become Byzantium's most characteristic art. In the niches adorning fountains in Pompeian courtyards, they must have produced scintillating effects in the strong sunshine.

The largest houses of all, known as "villas," were not inside the town itself, but in the surrounding countryside, where they provided rich men and women with luxury summer residences, with ample farms attached. The Villa of Publius

Fannius Sinistor at Boscoreale has soaring architectural vistas, and the Villa of the Mysteries has long been known for an extraordinary cycle of religious wall paintings connected with the Dionysiac rite; while the Villa of the Papyri, outside Herculaneum (imaginatively reconstructed as the J. Paul Getty Museum at Malibu in California), became famous for its astonishing yields both of literary papyri and ancient bronze statues. Recent researches have added enormously to the number of known villas throughout this entire area, so that they form one of the most active and productive fields of current study. For example, more than a dozen such mansions have come to light on the maritime hillside above Stabiae (Castellamare di Stabia), some three miles south of Pompeii. And now a very imposing villa, with substantial farm buildings and lands, has been discovered at Oplontis or Oplontiae (Torre Annunziata), three miles west of Pompeii; more than fifty of its rooms have been cleared, and a long, continuous colonnade facing south over the seashore. As happened in so many cases, extensive damage was caused to the villa by the earthquake of A.D. 62. Then, seventeen years later, the disastrous eruption buried the house under six feet of ash and pumice, topped by another fifteen of volcanic mud.

There is clearly more, much more, still to be found at these country villas. But indeed the same applies to Pompeii as a whole; two-fifths of the place remains to be discovered. Fortunately, excavation continues unabated. There have been notable recent discoveries not only at Stabiae, Oplontis and Herculaneum, but also in the central Pompeian zone itself, for instance at a vineyard just inside the walls of the town, in a necropolis in the outskirts, and at a number of the city's town houses as well, including those of Sallust (so-called) and Gaius Julius Polybius. The house of the latter, who owned inns and hotels in the city, has continued to yield finds of particular importance, including shortly before these lines were written, a collection of bronzes (among them, a notable statue of a young man), which is one of the most significant discoveries of recent years.

So let us hope that the red bowels of Vesuvius will not become aggressively explosive once again. It is not possible to be too optimistic on this point. Every month, the local observatory registers up to ten *microterremoti*, mini-earthquakes. Moreover, since A.D. 79, there have been no less than seventy eruptions—averaging one every twenty-seven years. The last of them took place in 1944, thirty-five years ago. It served as a reminder that the mountain was the only active volcano on the continent of Europe—and will someday, therefore, be heard of again, although the pause since the last outburst has been a long one. Moreover, when the next eruption comes, it is unlikely to be a negligible affair. The 1944 disturbance sealed the top of the crater down completely, removing the plume or pall of smoke which in many paintings of Vesuvius is shown hanging over the mountain. Next time, therefore, the seething underneath the earth will remain bottled up until the whole top is blown violently off, just as it was blown off in A.D. 79. As the novelist Charles Dickens declared, "the mountain is the genius of the scene, the doom and destiny of this beautiful country, biding its time."

Note. For readers who feel strong enough for a recipe for Pompeian fish-sauce, (*garum*), I repeat the version offered in my *Cities of Vesuvius.* "The entrails of sprats or sardines—the parts that could not be used for salting—were mixed with finely chopped portions of fish, and with roe and eggs, and then pounded, crushed and stirred. The mixture was left in the sun or in a warm room and beaten into a homogeneous pulp until it fermented. When this *liquamen,* as it was called, had been much reduced over a period of six weeks by evaporation, it was placed in a basket with a perforated bottom through which the residue filtered slowly down into a receptacle. This end-product, decanted into jars, was the famous *garum;* the dregs left over, also regarded as edible, were known as *allec.*"

Michael Grant

As one enters Pompeii, the town calls up a vision of civic activity, of crowds in the Forum, in the shops and main thoroughfares, of silence and peace in the secondary streets and private houses. Panels depicting villas and houses—often works of fantasy—are frequent in Pompeii and show the importance given to the role of architecture in a natural setting.

Above
Villa at the Seaside. A splendid villa maritima with porticoes running the whole length of the facade. From Stabiae. (Naples, National Museum).

Above
The interior of the *Basilica*, the large building at the southwest end of the Forum. Built toward the end of the 2nd century B.C., it was the main center for the administration of justice and business transactions.

Facing page
The Quadriporticus, also called the Doric Portico, behind the stage of the Great Theater, was built in the 2nd century B.C. as a shelter for spectators during intermissions between the acts of theatrical performances. After the earthquake of 62 A.D., the Quadriporticus was subjected to considerable alterations. Small rooms were built along the inner wall and the court was transformed into barracks for gladiators. This has been confirmed by many beautiful gladiatorial weapons discovered there.

The Thermopolium—shop selling hot food and drinks—in Via dell'Abbondanza (Abundance Street). In the foreground is the sales counter, with round openings in which food containers were inserted. At the far end is the Lararium, family shrine dedicated to ancestors and the protective geniuses of the house. Adjacent to the shop was the host's apartment, decorated with paintings.

Grinding Mills for the grain in a bakery (pistrinum). The grain was poured in at the top and the flour ran out at the base. Bread began to be made in Pompeii after the 2nd century B.C.; previously flour was used for making puls, a sort of porridge. The mills were ordinarily powered by mules, sometimes by slaves, or convicts.

Peristyle of the House of the Vettii. In the garden area are several sculptures, water basins and fountains, and the walls under the portico are decorated with paintings. Inside the house there are magnificent wall decorations. Bronze seals found in the house have identified the Vettii as a rich and powerful family of freedmen.

The mosaic and shell-decorated fountain in *nymphaeum of the House of the Great Fountain*. On each side of the fountain is a tragic mask in high relief. The bronze putto with dolphin is a cast of the original. In Roman houses, the nymphaeum—consisting of a niche with fountain, was dedicated to the nymphs and muses.

The basic *Plan of a Pompeian House* consists of the atrium surrounded by small rooms (cubicula) opening onto it; at the further end is a living room (tablinum), beyond which is a garden within high walls. From the 2nd century on this basic plan was extended by adding a dining room (triclinium) and peristyle.

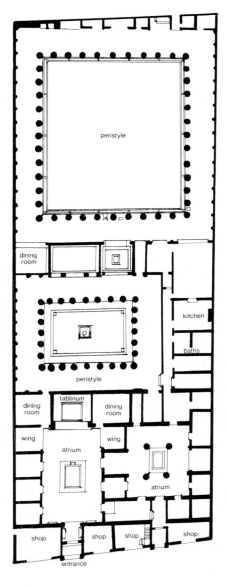

Above
Plan of the House of the Faun, one of the largest and most beautiful houses in Pompeii, with two atria, two triclinia and two peristyles.

Right
Two views of the *Nymphaeum in the house of Octavius Quartio,* Pompeii.

Plan labels (House of the Faun):
peristyle
dining room
kitchen
baths
peristyle
dining room
tablinum
dining room
wing
atrium
wing
atrium
shop
shop
shop
shop
entrance

House of the Neptune Mosaic, Herculaneum. A corner of the unroofed dining room (triclinium), with the niches of a nymphaeum on one side. The house is named after the large mosaic on the right, representing Neptune and Amphitrite under an arch of shell design. Rooms opening to the sky and balconies are frequent in villas at Herculaneum.

The Lararium of the House of Menander, with portrait busts of ancestors on a little altar.

Side Room off the Atrium in the House of the Vettii. In the center of large rectangular paintings simulating curtains are medallions with the heads of Medusa, satyrs and rams.

The most remarkable aspect of Pompeian houses is the resplendent decoration of their interiors, consisting of a wide variety of ornamental motifs and paintings. These decorations have been classified in four styles, according to chronology, techniques and the characteristics of their elements. Pompeian painting has great historical value because beyond the intrinsic quality of the work, it offers the only surviving examples of the tradition of ancient Greek painting.

This wall in the *Ixion Room,* one of the triclinia in the House of the Vettii, is a superb example of Fourth Style decoration. The large mythological painting on red ground depicts Daedalus presenting his wooden cow to Pasiphae. In the light-background panel at right are shown the figures of a satyr with the Hora of Summer soaring into the air.

Above: *Game Bird and Fruit,* and *Peaches with Glass Jar,* wall paintings from Herculaneum. (Naples, National Museum). Below: *Atys and a Nymph,* wall painting in the House of Pinarius Ceralis, Pompeii.

Facing page: *Ganymede Abducted by an Eagle,* stucco decoration on a vault of the Stabian Baths. This art form, also used in the decoration of private houses, reached a high level of development in Pompeii.

Left

Villa of Publius Fannius Sinistor, Boscoreale. Detail of a room, the walls of which are completely decorated with architectural fantasies and rural vistas between columns painted in trompe-l'oeil (New York, Metropolitan Museum of Art).

Below

Psychai Gathering Flowers, from the Frieze of the Crafts, detail of a mural decoration in the House of the Vettii, Pompeii. The fantastic architectonic decoration with candelabra, delicate plant forms and flowers is in the early Fourth Style.

Left
Apollo overcoming the Serpent Python, detail of mural decoration in the large garden room of the House of the Vettii. In the wall above the mythological scene rise fantastic architectonic decorations consisting of festive candelabra and slender herms on the black ground.

Facing page
Detail of elaborate *Scenographic Wall Decoration* in the Fourth Style from the Basilica in Herculaneum. (Naples, National Museum).

In sculpture, as in painting and other art forms, the Romans considered Greek art as a perfect model and source of inspiration. Their copies from Greek masterpieces, which often existed in several versions, make it possible in many cases to reconstruct lost originals and are essential for the study of Greek sculpture.

Facing page
Venus and Priapus, gilded marble from the House of Julia Felix, in Pompeii. Probably deriving from an original executed in Asia Minor ca. 200 B.C., this statue portrays the goddess preparing for the bath. She leans on a statuette of Priapus and a small Eros is seated at her feet. (Naples, National Museum).

Right
Head of a Boy, marble from the House of the Citharist, Pompeii. The boy has been identified as a member of the Popidii, one of the most powerful and wealthy families in Pompeii before the Roman colonization. (Naples, National Museum).

Left
Herm with the Head of Faunus, polychrome marble, from Pompeii. Faunus was the Roman deity of fields and flocks. These rectangular pillars—commonly endowed with male attributes and surmounted by a human head—were originally dedicated to the god Hermes, hence the appellation "herm." They were frequently placed in gardens and at crossroads as protection from evil spirits. (Naples National Museum).

Facing page, left
Apollo Citharist, bronze from the House of the Citharist, Pompeii. The statue is a copy of a mid-5th century B.C. original and was made in the second half of the 1st century B.C. The god is holding a plectrum in his right hand; and the left was probably used to hold a torch. (Naples, National Museum).

Facing page, right
The Doryphoros, or Spear Bearer, marble, from the Samnite Palaestra in Pompeii. This over-life-size copy from the 5th-century B.C. original by Polycleitos dates from ca. 70 B.C. and stood on a pedestal in the Palaestra. It is supposed to have carried a spear in the left hand. (Naples, National Museum).

42

Below center
Scene from a Comedy, terracotta relief, one of the few known depictions of the comic genre. The scene exemplifies the lively mimic acting of Roman comedy. The provenance of this piece is unknown, but reliefs from Pompeii and Herculaneum show similar comic masks. (Farnese Collection; Naples, National Museum).

Below
Putto with Goose, bronze, one of several statuettes found in the peristyle of the House of the Vettii.

Scenes of daily life
on domestic walls

Pompeians, like the Romans, appear to have been greatly interested in recording the events of their day, as revealed by themes of everyday life in paintings decorating their houses.

Facing page
Brawl between Pompeians and Nucerians in the Amphitheater, detail of mural painting from the House of the gladiator Actius Anicetus, Pompeii. The picture depicts a nortorious episode in Pompeian history, when, in 59 A.D. a violent altercation took place during a gladiatorial combat in the Amphitheater, between Pompeians and their neighbors the Nucerians. The violence of the fight resulted in many casualties, some fatal, and the Amphitheater was closed for a number of years. (Naples, National Museum).

Below
Chariot Race, detail of a mural painting from the House of the Chariots(?), Pompeii. The painting depicts four four-horse chariots (quadrigae) in the arena. Chariot racing and gladiatorial combats were the most popular sports in the Roman era. (Naples, National Museum).

Above

The Sorceress and the Traveler, also called The Water Seller,
detail of mural painting from the House of the Dioscuri,
Pompeii. Because of widespread magic, occultism, and
superstition in Pompeii, the Roman Senate instituted laws against
sorcerers, soothsayers and astrologers, who were considered a
menace to the State. (Naples, National Museum).

Below

The Banquet, detail of a Fourth-Style mural painting from the triclinium of a house in Pompeii, whose owner is portrayed with his guests, attended by young slaves. At lower right a slave is supporting one of the guests who appears to have had too much to drink. (Naples, National Museum).

Facing page
The Tragic Actor, detail of mural painting from Herculaneum. Probably a copy from a Hellenistic prototype, the painting represents an actor after the play. He has removed his mask and is looking at a woman—an admirer or muse—who is writing a dedicatory inscription. Another actor behind is taking off his costume. (Naples, National Museum).

Above
Double Portrait of a Magistrate and His Wife, mural painting from a house in Pompeii which was supposed to have belonged to the baker Terentius Proculus and his brother, the magistrate Terentius Neo. The symbols of learning—the scroll, the wax tablet and the stylus—would indicate this to be the portrait of the magistrate and his wife. (Naples, National Museum).

The Bakery, detail of mural painting from Pompeii. It represents the free distribution of bread made by an official during election times in order to gain popularity, as confirmed by the attitude and elegance of the figure behind the counter. The loaves depicted are identical with some actually found in excavations. (Naples, National Museum).

Above

Argument in a Caupona, detail of a mural painting found in a tavern (caupona) in Mercury Street, Pompeii. The man standing near the table seems to be arguing with the seated one, who is drinking. Two other men, probably waiters, intervene to settle the quarrel. (Naples, National Museum).

Dreams of legend and myth:
The ancient themes of painting

Mythological themes provided a conspicuous source of inspiration for Pompeian wall painters. Although imitating Greek originals, these subjects are interpreted quite freely and imaginatively.

Facing page
Ulysses Listening to the Sirens' Song, detail of a mural painting from Pompeii. The setting of the Sirens' cliffs past which Ulysses' boat is sailing is rendered with staccato accents of form, color and movement. (Naples, National Museum).

Below
Mythological Scene, one of a series of mural paintings decorating a gallery in the House of the Cryptoporticus. The picture is of a type called *pinax,* with shutters illusionistically painted at each side. The subject represents Alcestis' farewell to her husband, with Charon waiting for her in his boat.

Above

Centaur with Citharist, detail of a mural decoration from a
wall in the Villa of Cicero, Pompeii, outside the Herculaneum
Gate on Via dei Sepolchri. Composed with extreme elegance
on its black background, the group belongs to a late phase of
the Third Style, dating from the middle of the 1st century B.C.
(Naples, National Museum).

Above

Bacchante Taming a Centaur, another beautiful detail from the wall decoration in the Third Style, in the series from the Villa of Cicero. The lively group shows the Bacchante grasping the centaur's hair at the back of his neck, and holding a thyrsus as a whip in the other hand. (Naples, National Museum).

Top
Sacrifice to Diana, with figures bringing offerings to an altar.

Above
Cupids as Wine Merchants, from the frieze of the Crafts and
Trades. Details of wall decorations in the Fourth Style in the
House of the Vettii, Pompeii.

Facing page
The Three Graces, Fourth Style painting derived from Hellenistic
prototypes. From Stabiae (Naples, National Museum).

56

Above

The Finding of Telephus, mural painting from the Basilica in Herculaneum. Telephus, the future founder of Pergamum, is discovered and recognize by his father. The seated figure personifies Arcadia. (Naples, National Museum).

Facing page

Young Satyr Dancing, detail of wall painting in a small room in the Villa of the Mysteries, Pompeii. The naked figure with mischievous grin, arm akimbo and leg raised in a mock dance faces a drunken Silenus on the opposite wall.

The Dionysiac mysteries

Details of the frieze decorating the "Room of the Mysteries," the meaning of which has never been conclusively explained. Undoubtedly connected with the Dionysiac-Bacchic myth, the painting could be a portrayal of a mimed satire narrating episodes from the Dionysiac legend. The series constitutes the greatest surviving example of ancient painting. In deriving his figures from Greek originals, the unknown painter of this work displays an extraordinary ability to convey the idea of a world which blends the human with the divine.

Facing page, above
A Priestess Seated at a Table is assisted by two helpers, while the aged Silenus plays a lyra.

Lower left
A Young Satyr Playing a Syrinx watches a female satyr suckling a young goat; the terror-stricken woman at their side is the wind nymph Aula.

Below center
A Boy, Probably the Young Dionysus, is reading from a scroll, tenderly assisted by a woman, perhaps his mother Semele; another woman wearing a crown of olive leaves, carries a tray of sacrificial cakes.

Below right
The Anxiously Watching Woman sitting on a couch has been variously interpreted as the bride or the mother of the bride.

Details from the great frieze of the Dionysiac myth in the Villa of the Mysteries, Pompeii:

Above
Young Satyr Playing a Syrinx, detail of plate, p. 60.

Facing page
A Young Woman Nude to the Waist, probably the initiate, is being comforted by a priestess; in the background at right of the group is a bacchante holding a thyrsus.

One of the most characteristic and successful arts of the Roman world was mosaic, used almost exclusively as floor decoration, functioning as an ornamental element like a rug. The mosaic often had a central panel known as the emblema, which had some realistically rendered pictorial theme.

Above
Alexander and Darius at the Battle of Issus, mosaic from the floor of the exedra, opening onto the smaller peristyle in the House of the Faun. This remarkable mosaic is a copy from a Greek painting of the 4th century B.C., probably by Philoxenes of Eretria. (Naples, National Museum).

Left
Emblema with the Symbols of Life and Death, mosaic found in the triclinium of an apartment connected with the Tannery, in Pompeii.

Facing page
Women Consulting a Sorceress, mosaic from the Villa of Cicero, Pompeii. The work is signed by Dioscurides of Samos, but it is not known whether he was the author of the mosaic or of the painting from which it was copied. (Naples, National Museum).

Facing page
Portrait of a Lady, mosaic emblema from a
house in Pompeii depicting a young woman
of a rich family, as indicated by the jewelry
and the dress she is wearing. (Naples,
National Museum).

Right
Venus Doing up her Sandal, an example of
inlaid polychrome marble called *opus sectile,*
from Pompeii. (Naples, National Museum).

Pp. 68–69
Rehearsal for a Greek Satyr Play, mosaic
emblema from the House of the Tragic
Poet, Pompeii. The seated bald man is
directing the actors in steps to the music
played by the figure with double-pipes; to
the right, one actor is donning a costume.
(Naples, National Museum).

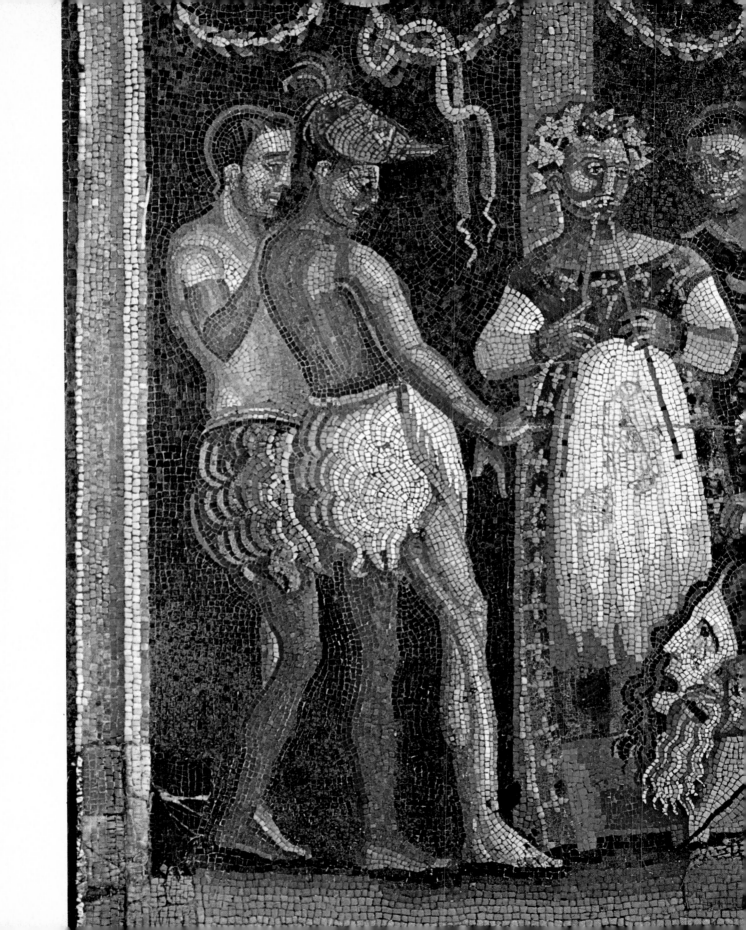

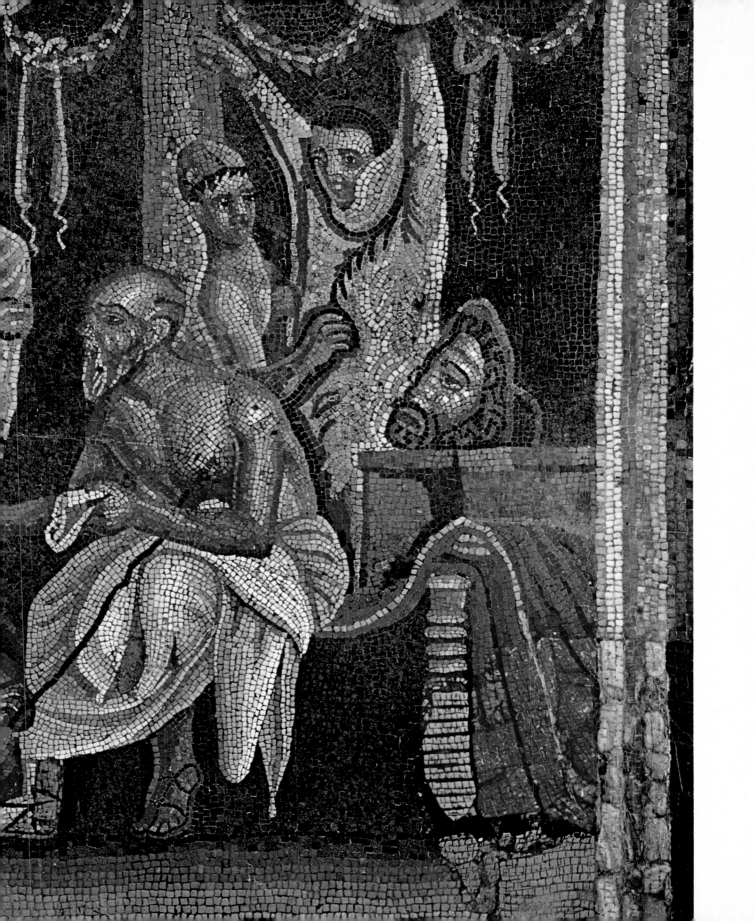

Cat Devouring a Partridge, and Ducks with Birds and Fish, mosaic emblema from the House of the Faun. (Naples, National Museum).

Sea Creatures, mosaic emblema from Pompeii. The graphic realism is
due to the very small tesserae employed. (Naples, National Museum).

Refined taste for precious objects:
Glass, jewels and the noble metals

The numerous objects of fine and costly workmanship found in Pompeii reflect the refined taste not only of the rich but of the population at large. Precious materials were widely used and often art objects of exceptional craftsmanship were imported from famous centers, not only in Italy, but from the Mediterranean world as far as Egypt or the Near East.

Facing page

Amphora with Putti, detail of a blue-glass amphora from a tomb on the Via dei Sepolcri, Pompeii. The technique of this decoration—showing putti harvesting grapes—is similar to that of cameos. Dating from the second quarter of the 1st century A.D., this piece was probably not produced in Pompeii, where craftsmanship of this type did not reach such a level of quality. (Naples, National Museum).

Below

Three Pitchers and a Chalice of Blue Glass from Pozzuoli, found in a house in Pompeii. Glass objects such as these were often modeled from similar versions in precious metals. (Naples, National Museum).

Gold jewelry found in Pompeii:

Top
Bracelet in the form of a serpent with ruby head.

Middle left
Gold Bulla from the House of Menander, a type of jewel worn by Roman children of free birth.

Middle right
Ring with a Man's Profile engraved on a carnelian.

Right
Bracelet of Hollow Gold Hemispheres. (Naples,

Facing page
A series of *Pompeian earrings,* of which those with spherical segments in gold inserted with carnelians (center) and those with bunches of pearls (lower right) are from the House of Menander. (Naples, National Museum).

Right

Bronze Apparatus for Heating Liquids, from Stabiae. The liquid—wine, water or any other—was poured into the cylindrical container on the left, from which it passed into the hollow wall of the round fire-box. The hot liquid could then be drawn off through the tap at right.

Below

Sistrums and Cymbals found in the Temple of Isis, in Pompeii. The sistrum, a bronze loop crossed by rods producing a tinkling sound when shaken, was used by worshippers of Isis during rituals. The cymbals, disks also of bronze, were beaten rhythmically during religious functions. (Naples, National Museum).

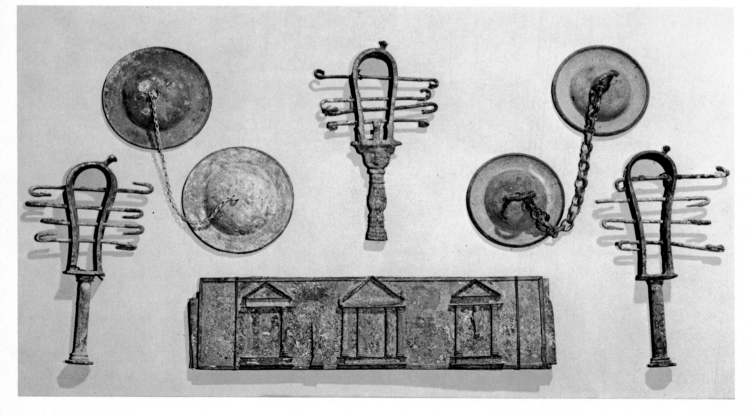

Left
Bronze Wind Instrument probably for playing during religious ceremonies.

Above
Bronze tripod with young fauns. Three slender ithyphallic fauns support a lebes, or basin, in the form of a basket. Found in a house in Pompeii, this astonishing tripod dates from the early Empire. (Naples, National Museum).

Right
Gladiator's Bronze Helmet,
decorated with the Roman eagle

Below left
Silver Dipper with handle decorated
with the head of Medusa.

Below right
Silver dish for fruit or cakes in the
shape of a shell; both these objects
are from the House of Menander in
Pompeii. (Naples, National
Museum).

Opposite page, above
Silverware from Pompeii and from
sites in the Vesuvian area.

Opposite page, below
Surgical Instruments in bronze and
iron. (Naples, National Museum).

Above
Silver Mirror-back decorated with the head of a young woman
in relief. Found in the House of Menander in Pompeii
(Naples, National Museum).

Left

One of a Pair of Roman Drinking Cups, or kantharoi, from the luxurious dinner service of the House of Menander, decorated with olive branches in high relief, dating from the Augustan age. (Naples, National Museum).

Below

Silver Cup with Cupids Riding Centaurs. Two sides of a kantharus from the treasure consisting of 118 pieces of magnificent silverware found in an underground chamber of the House of Menander. These pieces, together with the treasure of over one hundred embossed silver vessels found at Villa La Pisanella at Boscoreale reveal the wealth and refined taste of Pompeians together with the high level of craftsmanship of local silversmiths. (Naples, National Museum).

INDEX OF ILLUSTRATIONS

BIBLIOGRAPHY

G. FIORELLI: *Gli Scavi di Pompei dal 1861 al 1872.* Napoli, 1873.

E. BULWER-LYTTON: *The Last Days of Pompeii.* London, 1834.

J. SOGLIANO: *Gli Scavi di Pompei dal 1873–1900.* Roma, 1904.

MUSEO NAZIONALE DI NAPOLI: *Pitture murali e mosaici nel Museo Nazionale di Napoli.* Roma, 1932.

E. PERNICE: "Pavimente und figürliche Mosaiken," in *Die hellenistische Kunst in Pompei,* VI. Berlin, 1938.

R. BIANCHI-BANDINELLI, "Tradizione ellenistica e gusto romano nella pittura pompeiana," in *La critica d'arte,* 1941.

C. M. DAWSON: *Roman-Campanian Mythological Landscape Painting.* New Haven, 1944.

A. MAIURI: *L'ultima fase edilizia di Pompei.* Roma, 1942.

————. *Pompei ed Ercolano tra case e abitanti.* Padova, 1950.

A. DE FRANCISCIS: *Il ritratto romano a Pompei.* Napoli, 1951.

K. SCHEFOLD: *Pompejanische Malerei, Sinn und Ideengeschichte.* Basel, 1952.

M. M. GABRIEL: *Masters of Campanian Painting.* New York, 1952.

A. MAIURI: *Roman Painting.* Geneva, 1953.

P. W. LEHMANN: *Roman Wall Paintings from Boscoreale in the Metropolitan Museum of Art.* Cambridge, Mass., 1953.

K. SCHEFOLD: *Die Wande Pompejis,* Berlin, 1957.

G. O. ONORATO: *Iscrizioni pompeiane: La vita publica.* Firenze, 1957.

A. & B. MAIURI: *Museo Nazionale di Napoli.* Novara, 1957.

R. SIVIERO: *Jewelry and Amber of Italy: A Collection in the National Museum of Naples.* New York, 1959.

M. BRION: *Pompeii and Herculaneum.* New York, 1960.

A. MAIURI: *Pompei, Ercolano, e Stabia, le citta sepolte dal Vesuvio.* Novara, 1961.

M. BIEBER: *The History of the Greek and Roman Theater.* Princeton, 1961.

A. DE FRANCISCIS: *Il Museo Nazionale di Napoli.* Cava dei Tirreni, 1963.

C. L. RAGGHIANTI: *Pittore di Pompei.* Milano, 1963.

R. ETIENNE: *La Vie Quotidienne à Pompei.* Paris, 1966.

A. DE FRANCISCIS: *La pittura pompeiana.* Firenze, 1968.

W. LEPPMANN: *Pompeii in Fact and Fiction.* London, 1968.

M. GRANT: *Cities of Vesuvius: Pompeii and Herculaneum.* London, 1971.

M. GRANT, A. DE SIMONE, M. T. MERELLA: *Eros a Pompei.* Milano, 1974.

T. KRAUS: *Pompeii and Herculaneum, the Living Cities of the Dead.* New York, 1975.

E. LA ROCCA, M. & A. DE VOS, AND F. COARELLI: *Guida di Pompei,* Milano, 1976.

R. TREVELYAN: *The Shadow of Vesuvius: Pompeii A. D. 79.* London, 1976.

CREDITS